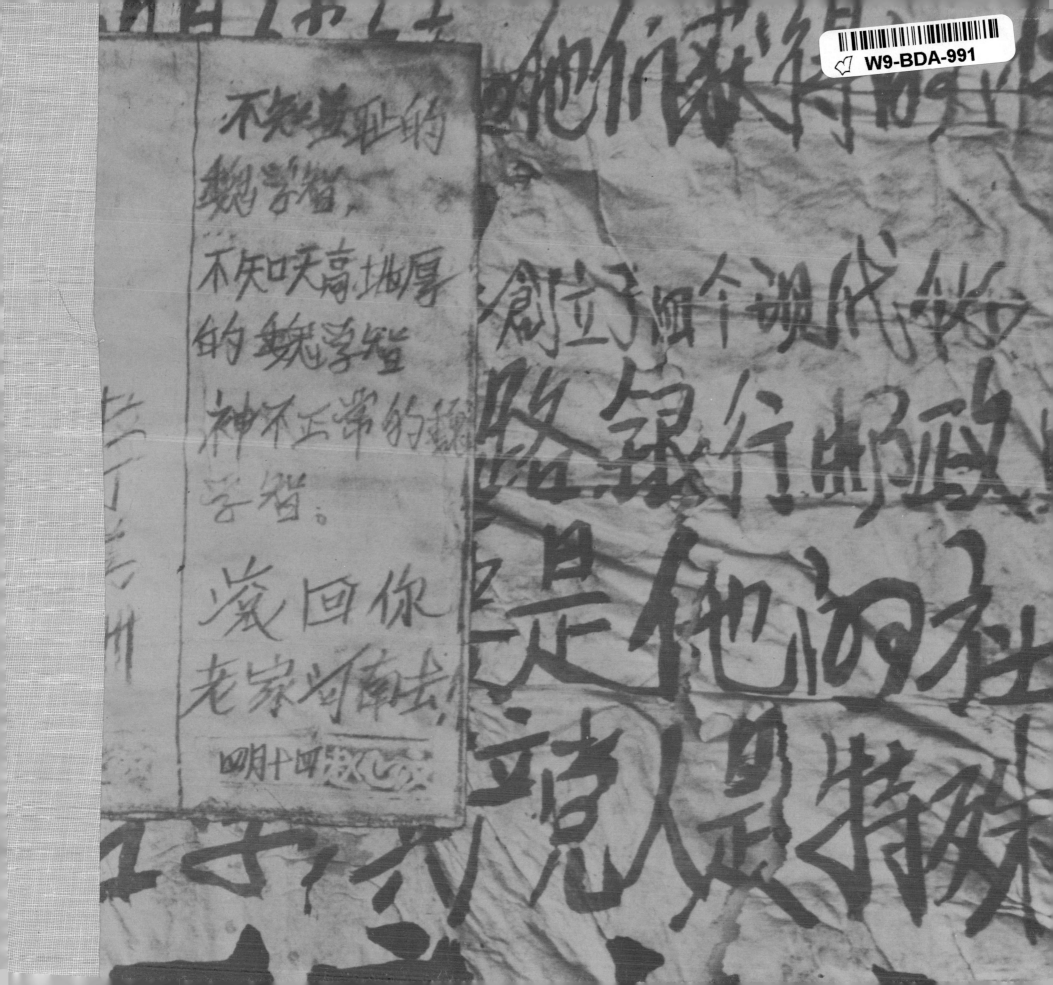

不知羞耻的
魏学智，
不知天高地厚
的魏学智
神不正常的魏
学智。
滚回你
老家河南去！

ALSO BY MARC RIBOUD:

Three Banners of China

The Face of North Vietnam

VISIONS OF CHINA

VISIONS OF CHINA

PHOTOGRAPHS BY MARC RIBOUD 1957 - 1980

INTRODUCTION BY ORVILLE SCHELL

PANTHEON BOOKS   NEW YORK

ENGLISH TRANSLATION COPYRIGHT © 1981 BY RANDOM HOUSE, INC.
INTRODUCTION COPYRIGHT © 1981 BY ORVILLE SCHELL
ALL RIGHTS RESERVED UNDER INTERNATIONAL AND PAN-AMERICAN COPYRIGHT CONVENTIONS.
PUBLISHED IN THE UNITED STATES BY PANTHEON BOOKS, A DIVISION OF RANDOM HOUSE, INC., NEW YORK,
AND SIMULTANEOUSLY IN CANADA BY RANDOM HOUSE OF CANADA LIMITED, TORONTO.
ORIGINALLY PUBLISHED IN FRANCE AS CHINE: INSTANTANÉS DE VOYAGES BY ARTHAUD.
COPYRIGHT © 1980 BY LES EDITIONS ARTHAUD, PARIS.
LIBRARY OF CONGRESS CATALOGING IN PUBLICATION DATA
RIBOUD, MARC.
VISIONS OF CHINA.
TRANSLATION OF CHINE.
1. CHINA—DESCRIPTION AND TRAVEL—1949—1975—VIEWS.
2. CHINA—DESCRIPTION AND TRAVEL—1976—VIEWS.
I. TITLE.
DS711.R4813   951.05   80-8645
ISBN 0-394-51535-8
ISBN 0-394-74840-9 (PBK.)
CAPTIONS TRANSLATED BY MARY FEENY
MANUFACTURED IN THE UNITED STATES OF AMERICA
FIRST AMERICAN EDITION

INTRODUCTION

Like astronomers looking through the eyepiece of a telescope to divine the realities of galaxies light-years away, most Westerners drawn to China have had to deal with the object of their curiosity from a distance. Since 1949, journalistic and photographic accounts have all too often simply glanced off China's surface.

What seemed to frustrate outsiders' attempts to probe the depths of the Chinese Revolution was much more than the physical inaccessibility of China to the Western world (although that was part of it). Even when writers and photographers succeeded in reaching China, they found themselves separated from daily life by impenetrable if often invisible barriers.

On tours of China, one often had the sense of being sequestered in a germ-free capsule, virtually guaranteeing no infectious contact between the Chinese people and their foreign visitors. Rather than allow for spontaneous and telling experiences to develop, the Chinese substituted speeches filled with statistics, films, banquets, and perfunctory tours through factories, schools, bomb shelters, and irrigation projects.

When foreign writers returned home to crank out an obligatory book or article about their visit, there were all too many paragraphs prefaced with, "We were told that...," as if the revolutionary experience of the country could be discerned from oracular statements of the endless, dreaded "brief introductions," which prefaced every new stop regardless of the hour and state of collapse of the weary traveler.

When foreign photographers returned home, hundreds of rolls of film often produced nothing more than technically good but unrevealing shots of smiling workers and peasants, endearing children, stone bridges, people riding bicycles, workers sitting at lathes, or the Great Wall disappearing over the mountainsides into the mist. Such photos had an unsatisfying flatness which may have suggested well enough how China looked to a visitor but missed the political energy and contradictions that actually animated the country. Too many of these photos gave the impression of having been shot out of the windows of buses and trains.

It is true that the Chinese have traditionally had a strong resistance to mingling too freely with those whom they have come to categorize as "foreign guests." Unlike the United States, China has never aspired to be a melting pot. China's rulers have often viewed foreign intrusions into their own civilization not as a source of hybrid vigor but of undesirable cross-cultural miscegenation. The disruptive impact of foreigners meddling in Chinese affairs has more than once triggered a reaction akin to tissue rejection.

While this strong traditionalist impulse to repel foreign intruders undeniably still exists, there is also, I think, a new aspect to Chinese opaqueness that derives from Maoism rather than isolationist Confucianism.

Heady from their success in "liberating" all of China in 1949, certain of China's leaders, Mao among them, hoped that their country's march into the communist millennium was now invincible. During 1958, the high tide of the Great Leap Forward, for example, the Chinese announced that they detected the first tender green "shoots" of communism beginning to appear as a result of the communization of the peasantry. Even the Russians did not pretend to have advanced beyond the stage of adolescent socialism in their march toward communism, and here the upstart Chinese, their revolutionary juniors, were proclaiming victory at hand.

Mao exhorted his fellow comrades on with such a sense of expectation and insistent optimism that there was little room for doubters troubled by the complexities of transforming one of the world's oldest and most traditional societies. During cataclysmic movements like the Great Leap Forward and the Cultural Revolution, it became unthinkable that the

Chinese Revolution, under the infallible leadership of Chairman Mao, would not bring a glorious new peasant paradise to term. A climate of such dogmatic revolutionary optimism was created that when failure did mar the landscape or delays did intrude upon the communist timetable, there was little public evidence of it. A combination of willed blindness and a fear of being branded counterrevolutionary kept most people silent. Those who did dissent from Mao's chiliastic thinking soon found themselves bulldozed aside.

Mistakes, failures, wrong judgments, were quickly obscured by a concealing web of official propaganda, so that the reality of what was actually going on became hopelessly blurred behind a system of reportage that could not speak unless it was announcing success. It was difficult enough even for ordinary Chinese to separate the mythology of the revolution from its actual accomplishments. At least they were able to judge (however silently) the concrete signs of the revolution progressing (or retrogressing) in their daily lives. But for most foreign visitors, kept at arm's length, the shadows and echoes produced by the official propaganda organs of the state provided a meager and often distorting reflection of what was really happening.

There was virtually no personal form of communication between Chinese and outsider. In addition, those impersonal forms of discourse which people have traditionally relied on to communicate across national boundaries—art, literature, theater, music, dance—had become so thoroughly a part of the official smokescreen that, except to the most discerning eye, they revealed little.

China's leaders were determined to purge all ambiguity, nuance, or sign of human frailty from the image of their revolution, just as they would shortly tint and rouge Mao's own corpse and enshrine it like a piece of waxed fruit beneath its crystal sarcophagus in Tiananmen Square. Like the public relations men whom they reviled in the countries of their capitalist enemies, China's leaders expended untold energy to expunge any suggestion of imperfection from their product.

As a result, from a distance the official Chinese Revolution seemed to have defied the laws which kept all other human endeavors in a state of compromise. From closer quarters, however, the lack of spontaneity and warmth of its images suggested a carefully directed theatrical, calculated to divert the audience's attention away from a tempestuous but hidden drama being played out backstage. For Western visitors, it was of course virtually impossible to get beyond this scripted performance to where the darker and more contradictory currents of life flowed.

Even in retrospect, it is still hard to pin down just what it was that drove the Chinese to spend so much obsessive energy on making their revolution seem more unerring than it was. Doubtless much of their Herculean effort derived from a genuine belief in Mao's vision of a new China, reborn, strong, proud, and united by the vision of an egalitarian future. Indeed, by 1949, the Chinese had "stood up," as Mao announced proudly from Peking's Gate of Heavenly Peace. Not only had they vanquished the forces of Chiang Kai-shek's Nationalist armies, but they had at last excised all the emissaries of Western imperialism who had controlled so much of China for so long.

Though China was officially "liberated," its new leaders seemed to find it necessary to indulge again and again in an unnatural totalism to prove the efficacy of their revolution. However, one sensed self-doubt just behind the bravado and revolutionary machismo that marked much of Communist China's last thirty years. The Chinese government's unwillingness to acknowledge its fallibility suggested a certain lack of confidence that could be disguised only with bluster.

Perhaps it has been China's unusually deep sense of wounded national pride that has provoked its leaders into such escalating panegyrics about their revolution. It was certainly true that the needs of their people created a sense of urgency and put a premium on achieving quick results; but it was the judgmental gaze of the world, and particularly of the West, which heightened the process. With their former Western conquerors and enemies endlessly predicting the failure of Mao's new social experiments, the leaders of what was once the "sick man of Asia" doubtless found it doubly difficult to admit to anything but resounding success.

China treated the vagaries of its social transformation as an essentially private affair, evincing a certain shyness toward the outside world. It was not unlike a youth entering puberty. Rather than reveal his doubts in public, he instead makes bravado claims to suggest that the process of his becoming a man is somewhat ahead of where it might actually be.

Although Mao tirelessly proclaimed the revolutionary process as "permanent," one which could never end, he was also an impatient man who wanted results fast. Lieutenants who were cowed by his voracious appetite for progress often settled for the appearance of results rather than for the results themselves. Even though China might not always live up to the expectations of the moment, it was the unspoken obligation of all good comrades to temporarily hide discrepancies between theory and practice until the two could at last be brought into parallel.

When the dead weight of China would not change fast enough or conform to the ambitious revolutionary schedule of its leaders, one could at least create the semblance of momentum lest anyone have reason to doubt the efficacy of Mao Zedong Thought. When economic statistics were not sufficiently impressive, or when economic growth rates did not reflect well on "putting politics in command," the temptation to alter the figures a little so as not to defile the public record with unseemly setbacks was often overpowering. In the end, when China would spring forth from its protective cocoon of propaganda as a fully developed nation to dazzle the world, it would have all been worth it. People would understand the massaging of reality as an excusable means to a worthy end.

In a society so traditionally ethnocentric and militantly caught up in the question of appearances, only the most discerning foreign visitor could see through the camouflaged surface to the involved world of tensions and contradictions below. Such a man is the French photographer Marc Riboud. Through his extraordinary photography, we are able to see past the rhetoric and polemics into the interior of Chinese life. His photographic narrative—which covers almost a quarter of a century—also gives us an almost electrocardiogram-like record of the twists and turns of recent Chinese political history.

Unlike any other series of photographs or even journalistic accounts, Riboud's collection graphically illustrates how the pendulum-like motion of Peking politics swept the Chinese people up in rising and falling tides of contradictory political movements. From periods of liberal moderation before the wilting of the Hundred Flowers (1956), exemplified by his photo of a young male sculptor working off a nude model, we are moved to a period of leftist radicalism with a Diane Arbus-like shot of a phalanx of militant young Chinese women marching in lock step just before the Cultural Revolution (1965).

From a 1965 photograph of a young man clenching his fist, his face twisted in a frenzy of revolutionary fervor before placards of Chairman Mao and Ho Chi Minh, Riboud moves us to 1980 and a photo of a cocky youth in a foreign-style felt hat, sleeveless sweater, and dark glasses, obviously aping the fashions of China's former capitalist-imperialist enemies.

A photo of a captive mock Uncle Sam being paraded through the streets at gunpoint by a youth dressed up as a defiant peasant contrasts stunningly with an absolutely marvelous shot of a Chinese photographer set up for business inside the Forbidden City, using a foreign black limousine as a backdrop for photos of Chinese tourists.

Riboud shows the inconsistencies and points of tension in the Chinese Revolution, not to deride it but to restore to it the humanity stripped from it for so long by the monotony of political propaganda. There is in his work irony, humor, anger, gladness, beauty, even some sordidness…all of the contradictory forces which have in fact animated China these last three decades. For Riboud, China appears as a fascinating universe of contrasts rather than a series of monochromatic tableaux. For me, it is the first collection of photos that has brought the People's Republic of China to life.

Not since the late 1940s, when Henri Cartier-Bresson photographed China poised on the edge of communist takeover, has anyone portrayed the Chinese with such mastery.

—ORVILLE SCHELL

PHOTOGRAPHER'S NOTE

This is a picture book. I am a photographer, not a Sinologue. In China I did a lot of walking, a lot of looking, and I took a lot of pictures. I also drank a lot of tea while listening to endless recitations of the latest versions of the Party doctrine. I read all the right books, learned what I could from fellow travelers, shared their enthusiasms, disappointments, and bewilderments. What else could I possibly add? To understand how the Chinese think and feel is so difficult that I leave the subtle art of analysis and commentary to others. The best way to discover China is perhaps to use one's eyes. Intense attention to detail and to the moment, here even more than elsewhere, can lead to knowledge and understanding.

For so long, and until so recently, China was a closed and secret land where the huge transformations taking place were almost always hidden from foreign eyes. Today the doors are opening. Visitors are flooding in. After a first impression of uniformity, of omnipresent poverty, they discover a mosaic of images where past and present, centuries-old traditions and the grip of the Party, are superimposed like double and triple exposures, rarely harmonizing, constantly clashing. That is why the photographs in this book are in no particular chronological or geographical order. I wanted them to confront and complete one another, thus reflecting today's China—like visual clues to better understand the present, to

better understand rather than to judge. Everywhere I saw and came to love the beauty of faces, the strange immensity of the landscapes. I sensed a dignity that has so often replaced humiliation.

In 1957, I had hardly stepped out of Peking Station when I took my first photograph (24): a broken-down rickshaw flanked by a ludicrous parasol: an image of the destitution left over from China's pre-revolution days.

In 1965, deep in the countryside, I saw students by the thousands (9 and 10) awkwardly wielding picks and shovels. They were forced to work off the temptations of city life and to cleanse themselves of the sin of intellectuals' pride.

In 1980, the last image of China I took away with me: in the heart of the Forbidden City, the Chinese no longer pose in front of Mao's portrait but beside a car, symbol of the consumer society's ideal all over the world. This is a stunning turn. Does the average Chinese, molded by years of forced egalitarianism and religious austerity, have, after all, the same yearnings as his cousin in Hong Kong? This pristine purity, after having fascinated our Western minds, has been discarded by the Chinese themselves. To dream of cars and gadgets is now authorized…but to dream only.

Mao's revolutionary drive ended in the Great Cultural Revolution. Where will this new surge of modernism and industrialization lead? If we go back and look at China again, we shall see.

— MARC RIBOUD

VISIONS OF CHINA

1. *Personality cult and pollution, Wuhan, 1971*

2. *Young pioneers on eve of the Cultural Revolution, Changchun, 1965*

3. *Suburbs of Peking, 1957*

4. *Peking subway station, 1979*

5. *Picasso's dove, Peking, 1957*

6. Students marching in slippered feet, Peking, 1965

7. *Impassioned support for Ho Chi Minh, Peking, 1965*

8. *Rally against the American presence in Vietnam, 1965*

9. *Intellectual in the fields, Hebei, 1965*

10. A group of "peasants," erstwhile students, Hebei, 1965

11. Poor peasant single-handedly hoeing wheat terraces, Shenxi, 1965

12. The jostle of collective labor, Hubei, 1965

13. Sowing potatoes, Heilongjiang, 1965

14. Rice fields, Sichuan, 1957

15. Wheat threshing, Gansu, 1957

16. A rare tractor, Hubei, 1965

17. Factory lunchroom, Peking, 1965

18. Tools and clothing out of the past, Guangxi, 1965

19. Students, Haerbin, 1965

20. *Fishermen on Li River, Guangxi, 1965*

21. Rice fields. Sichuan, 1957

22. *Transplanting rice by hand, Guangxi, 1965*

23. *Orders and slogans incite workers to produce, Anshan, 1965*

24. Rickshaw taxi, Peking, 1957

25. *Skating, Peking suburbs, 1965*

26. Snowstorm in the hutungs, *Peking, 1957*

27. *The Forbidden City, Peking, 1957*

28. *Schoolgirls, Peking, 1965*

29. *Father and son, Inner Mongolia, 1965*

30. *Patient being transported to the hospital, Sichuan, 1957*

31. Woman with bound feet, Peking, 1965

32. Ming dynasty bridge and dam, Sichuan, 1957

33. Wangfujing Street, Peking, 1979

34. Hunan, 1965

35. *Family lunch outside cave dwelling, Yanan, 1965*

36. *Peasant couple, Jiangsu, 1965*

37. *Lunch in a dirt-floored peasant home, Jiangsu, 1965*

38. *Fixing a guest "white tea," Sichuan, 1957*

39. *Traditional dress, The Forbidden City, Peking, 1957*

40. *Children with rented comics on a city street, Peking, 1965*

41. The Forbidden City, Peking, 1965

42. *Sunday outing, The Forbidden City, Peking, 1965*

43. *Street players, Peking, 1957*

44–47. *Street theater, Peking, 1957*

45.

46

47.

48. Wrestlers, Peking, 1957

49. *Woman, child, and Ming lion, Peking, 1965*

50. *Tai Ji Quan, The Forbidden City, Peking, 1957*

51. Chinese tourists, The Great Wall, 1971

52. *People's Liberation Army unit, The Great Wall, 1957*

53. Proud officer, Peking, 1965

54. *PLA violinist at Mayday festivities, Peking, 1965*

55. *PLA unit building a road to Vietnam, south of Nanning, 1965*

56. *Families, arbitrarily moved from their homes, arrive at station, 1957*

57. *University lecture hall, Kunming, 1965*

58. Reception at the Peking Hotel, 1957

59. Giant statue of Mao, Xian, 1971

60. Steel mill lunchroom, Anshan, 1957

61. Soviet-built ironworks, Anshan, 1965

62. *Foundry, Changchun, 1965*

63. *Storing blocks of ice for summer, Peking, 1957*

64. A Soviet expert, Wuhan, 1957

65. *"Switchboard," Anshan steel mill, 1965*

66. Cadres listening to superior, Yunnan, 1965

67. *Peasants learning to read, Gansu Province, 1957*

68. Anti-American demonstration, Peking, 1965

69. Dance at Peking University, 1957

70. *Reception for a Polish delegation, Peking, 1957*

71. Zhou Enlai, Peking, 1971

72. *Zhou Enlai, Peking, 1965*

73. *Teacups and revered ancestors, Peking, 1965*

74. *Divorce, Chinese-style, Peking, 1965*

75. *Apartment in housing project for workers, Changchun, 1965*

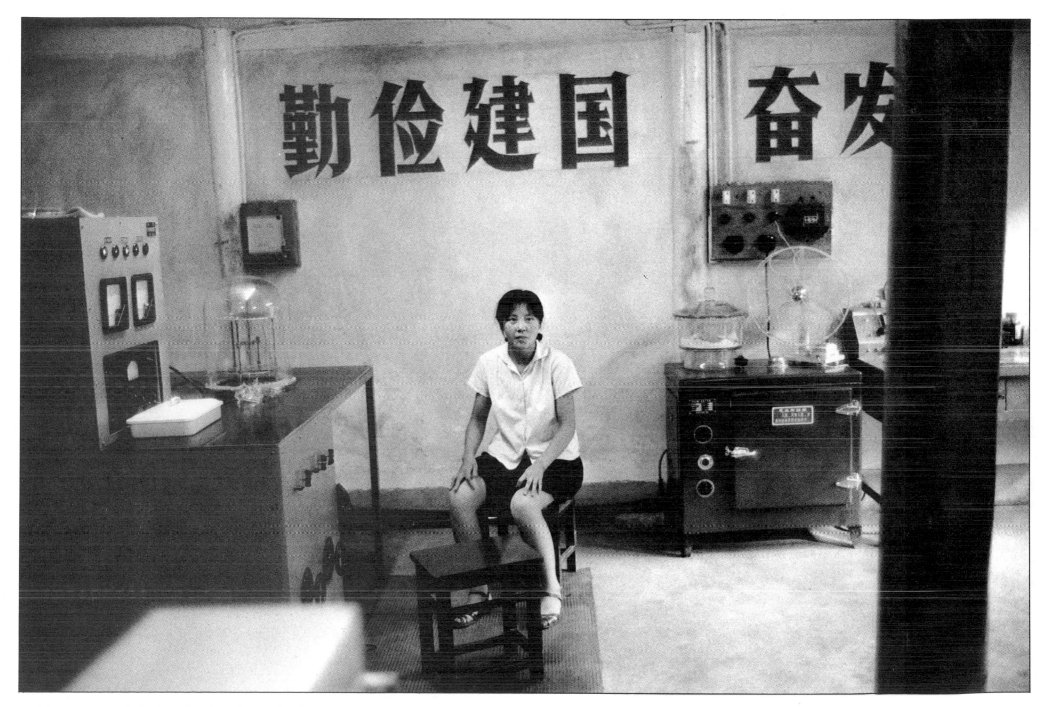

76. *Laboratory reopened after the Cultural Revolution, Shanghai, 1971*

77. Peking's largest hairdresser, 1979

78. *A wedding dance, Peking, 1957*

79. *Fine Arts Academy, Peking, 1957*

80. *Personality cult on a grand scale, Lanzhou, 1965*

81. *Propaganda poster, Shanghai, 1965*

82. Dazibaos *on the British Embassy walls, Peking, 1957*

83. Peasant woman, Henan, 1965

84–87. *Dazibaos on Democracy Wall, Peking, 1979*

85.

86.

87.

88. *Chinese toothpaste advertisement, Shanghai, 1979*

89. *Student dancer, Shanghai, 1971*

90. Posters, Peking, 1957

91. The antique dealers' street, Peking, 1965

92. *A rush to buy clothing, Peking, 1979*

93. *The price of duck causes consternation, Peking, 1965*

94. Young hooligans in women's hats, 1979

95. On the Bund, Shanghai, 1979

96. In the Hangzhou Gardens, 1979

97. *Survivor of the past, Peking, 1957*

98. *A girl captivated by her photographs, Suzhou, 1979*

99. Courting couple, Peking, 1979

100. *Discreet tête-à-tête, Shanghai, 1971*

101. PLA soldier standing guard, Peking, 1971

102. The Forbidden City, Peking, 1980

L I S T   O F   P H O T O G R A P H S

1. 1971. Wuhan. Personality cult and pollution. The Chinese are proud of the smoke from their factories; it symbolizes industrialization.

2. 1965. Changchun, on the eve of the Cultural Revolution. Well-drilled young pioneers like these will furnish the Red Guards with recruits.

3. 1957. Suburbs of Peking. Unpaved streets, quilted clothing, people still spontaneously friendly.

4. 1979. Peking subway station. The number of children in soldier suits shows how highly regarded the army is.

5. 1957. Peking. Picasso's dove. China was part of the Peace Movement at the time.

6. 1965. Peking's Tiananmen Square. These students marching in slippered feet are a sign of the Red Guard fury to come.

7. 1965. Peking during the Vietnam War. Impassioned support for Ho Chi Minh and the Vietnamese.

8. 1965. Demonstrations against the American presence in Vietnam. The caricature of Uncle Sam provokes outcry and insults.

9. 1965. Hebei Province. An intellectual sent to work in the fields, probably for several years, is banking a road.

10. 1965. Hebei Province. A group of "peasants," erstwhile students, awkwardly wielding picks and shovels.

11. 1965. This poor peasant single-handedly hoeing wheat terraces in Shenxi near Jinan harks back to pre-revolutionary China.

12. 1965. Hubei Province. The jostle of collective labor is the new daily rite in the countryside.

13. 1965. Heilongjiang Province, in the northeast. Sowing potatoes on a state-run farm.

14. 1957. In the Sichuan rice fields, the people's communes have not affected tradition. Even at work, women keep their children with them.

15. 1957. Gansu Province. Wheat threshing. Wheat is grown in the north, rice in the south.

16. 1965. Hubei Province. At this date, tractors were few and far between in China.

17. 1965. Peking suburbs. In factory lunchrooms, school cafeterias, and on state farms, the Chinese often eat standing up.

18. 1965. Guangxi Province. The rice fields have been converted to collective labor, but tools and clothing are out of the past.

19. 1965. Haerbin. Four women students with braided hair, which they will probably have to cut off during the Cultural Revolution.

20. 1965. In Guangxi, on the Li River near Guilin, the fishermen living on these boats constitute a people's commune.

21. 1957. In Sichuan, China's southwest, the most populous province and the largest rice producer, every square foot of land is farmed.

22. 1965. Guangxi's fertile rice fields are harvested twice a year. Transplanting is done by hand.

23. 1965. Anshan. Coolers in a heating plant near an ironworks. Orders and slogans incite workers to produce.

24. 1957. Peking. A rather unusual taxi in front of the train station. Today, rickshaws have disappeared.

25. 1965. Peking suburbs. Skating in the shadow of a pagoda and a factory. Physical fitness and industrialization were twin campaigns.

26. 1957. Peking. Snowstorm in the *hutungs*, the low-roofed old section of town.

27. 1957. Peking. The Forbidden City, which only the occasional snowstorm can empty of people. Closed during the Cultural Revolution, it is once again welcoming thousands of visitors.

28. 1965. Peking. Schoolgirls wear masks to protect themselves from the old section's dust as well as the mist.

29. 1965. Inner Mongolia. After a day of work on the steppes, a father and son go home to their tent dwelling.

30. 1957. In Sichuan, a patient is transported to the hospital. Sedan chairs were formerly reserved for the landowning class.

31. 1965. Peking. The Forbidden City. This woman still bears the mark of an old Chinese custom: she has trouble walking because her feet, bound when she was a child, are now hopelessly deformed.

32. 1957. Sichuan. A Ming dynasty bridge and stone dam, in a landscape shaped and farmed by human hands for centuries.

33. 1979. Peking's Wangfujing Street. These people are proud of their latest purchase: a television set, representing one year's wages.

34. 1965. Hunan Province. A profitable sale in the offing. These peasants have raised a sow on their own small plot of land and are now taking it to market.

35. 1965. Yanan in Shenxi Province. A family lunching in front of its cave dwelling, very near the one Mao lived in at the end of the Long March.

36. 1965. Jiangsu Province. For this peasant couple, the revolution has meant fuller rice bowls, electricity, and decent clothing.

37. 1965. Jiangsu Province. Lunch in a dirt-floored peasant home. At left, the bed with its mosquito netting.

38. 1957. Sichuan farm. Fixing a guest a glass of "white tea," that is, boiled water.

39. 1957. Peking. The Forbidden City. The traditional overcoat is vanishing, but old-style quilted black pants are still seen.

40. 1965. Peking. On a busy city street, children rent comics for a small sum.

41. 1965. Peking. The Forbidden City. The Chinese have a practical turn of mind, so children have slit pants.

42. 1965. Peking. In front of the white marble bridge at the gateway to the Forbidden City, a warmly dressed family in their Sunday best sets out for a stroll.

43. 1957. Outskirts of Peking. Street players perform in the traditional Peking Opera style. Improvised theater like this died out rapidly.

44–47. 1957. Peking. The Bridge of Heaven neighborhood. This is not a public punishment, but street theater. When the show is over, the actors pass the hat.

48. 1957. Peking. In the Bridge of Heaven neighborhood, now razed, two wrestlers entertain the locals.

49. 1965. Peking. A woman hoists her child onto a Ming lion in the old city.

50. 1957. Peking. The Forbidden City. Tai Ji Quan, the ancient, slow-motion military gymnastics, had many devotees. Today it is picking up again after the Cultural Revolution.

51. 1971. On Sunday, Chinese tourists flock to the Great Wall. The camera is a "Made in China" model.

52. 1957. A People's Liberation Army unit chose as its backdrop the Great Wall, the Middle Kingdom's rampart against barbarian invsions.

53. 1965. Peking. Proud of his uniform insignia, this officer poses for the photographer. Military rank was abolished soon afterwards.

54. 1965. Peking. Before the Cultural Revolution, Western music and the violin were not yet suspect. Here, a military band plays for the Mayday festivities.

55. 1965. South of Nanning, an army unit building a road to Vietnam leaves the work site with rifles, picks, shovels, and a quotation from Chairman Mao.

56. 1957. Arbitrarily moved from their homes in an eastern province, these families arrive at the station in the northwestern city of Lanzhou.

57. 1965. Kunming. In the university lecture hall, students wear masks to protect themselves from germs.

58. 1957. Peking. A reception at the Peking Hotel. Mao escorts the wife of Poland's premier. In the center, Marshal Zhu De, hero of the Long March.

59. 1971. Xian. A giant statue of Mao in front of the train station. Today's traveler will search for it in vain: it is no longer there.

60. 1957. Anshan. As elsewhere in China, it is hard to tell workers and engineers apart. Here, in a steel mill lunchroom, cadres wear their safety glasses even while eating.

61. 1965. Anshan. Rolling-mill of a Soviet-built ironworks. The Chinese worker's ingenuity makes up for flaws in Soviet automation.

62. 1965. Changchun. Foundry. The slogans appearing in all places of work encourage production.

63. 1957. Southern suburbs of Peking. With summer heat waves in mind, people cut blocks of ice and store them in a large hole during the winter.

64. 1957. Wuhan. A Soviet expert supervises the construction of a bridge on the Yangzi. Six years later, Krushchev recalled all Soviet advisers in China.

65. 1965. Anshan steel mill. The lack of a switchboard explains the presence of all the telephones in this engineer's office.

66. 1965. In a Yunnan people's commune, cadres obediently listen to a superior's directives.

67. 1957. In Gansu Province, illiterate peasants gather at an elementary school in the evening to learn to read.

68. 1965. Peking, on the Changan, or Lasting Peace Way. Millions of people file by, night and day, shouting anti-American slogans.

69. 1957. Dance at the University of Peking. The mask is to prevent the spread of germs. At any rate, kissing in public is unheard of.

70. 1957. Peking. Reception for a Polish delegation at the Peking Hotel. *Left,* Premier Zhou Enlai; *right,* a Polish diplomat's wife is initiated into the specialties of Chinese cuisine.

71. 1971. Peking. Premier Zhou Enlai during a conversation with Alain Peyrefitte, head of the French legislative delegation.

72. 1965. Peking. Premier Zhou Enlai during an interview with journalist K. S. Karol.

73. 1965. Peking. Cups of tea and portraits of revered ancestors: the ritual decor of all Chinese reception rooms.

74. 1965. Peking. Divorce, Chinese-style. After hearing out the grievances, the judges refuse to grant a divorce and recommend reconciliation.

75. 1965. Changchun. A two-room apartment in a housing project for workers. The family's most precious possessions are gathered in one corner of the bedroom: diplomas, photographs, alarm clock, and teapot.

76. 1971. Shanghai. Reopening a laboratory for measurement instruments at the university, closed during the Cultural Revolution.

77. 1979. Peking's largest hairdresser. The equipment dates back to pre-liberation days, but people line up for appointments just the same. A permanent wave is no longer considered a sin.

78. 1957. Peking. A wedding dance. Western dancing, permitted during the Hundred Flowers period and later during the spring of 1979, was recently banned again.

79. 1957. Peking, Fine Arts Academy. The surprises of the Hundred Flowers period swiftly yielded to Chinese and Maoist puritanism.

80. 1965. Lanzhou's main square. Personality cult on a grand scale.

81. 1965. Shanghai. The figures in propaganda posters always move triumphantly to the left.

82. 1957. Peking. On the walls of the British Embassy, *dazibaos,* or big character posters, condemn Anglo-French intervention in the Suez.

83. 1965. A peasant woman in Henan leaves a lunchroom, chopsticks in hand, reading *Young China.* The headline: "China Explodes Second Atomic Bomb."

84–87. 1979. Peking. Democracy Wall covered with *dazibaos.* The first on the left reads: "Let us banish this donkey dung [a pun on the name of the concerned party] from the People's Assembly."

88. 1979. Shanghai. Today, advertisements—for Chinese toothpaste or Japanese gadgets—are replacing the anti-imperialist slogans of yesteryear.

89. 1971. Shanghai. This student dancer catches up on required reading: the *Little Red Book.* Her only touch of fashion is Mao's insignia.

90. 1957. Peking. Posters for Chinese films and small businesses. They were prohibited during the Cultural Revolution but are making a comeback today.

91. 1965. Peking's Liulichang Street, the antique dealers' street, seen through the thoroughly Chinese doors and windows of a now-demolished shop.

92. 1979. Peking department store. A rush to buy clothing, which is still rationed.

93. 1965. Peking. At a market, the price of duck causes consternation. Lacquered duck remains a prized but expensive specialty.

94. 1979. Unable to pursue their studies because of the Cultural Revolution, young hooligans roam the streets in women's hats.

95. 1979. Shanghai. On the Bund. Little by little, work uniforms are being replaced by more elegant clothes.

96. 1979. In the Hangzhou Gardens. After forced egalitarianism of the Cultural Revolution, the desire to be different takes many forms.

97. 1957. Peking's Wangfujing Street. One of the last survivors of the past, aristocratic and proud of it.

98. 1979. Suzhou. After cycling through the rain to pick them up, a girl is captivated by her photographs.

99. 1979. Peking. Courting couples fill the park benches. Before they marry, the man must be 27, the woman 25.

100. 1971. Shanghai. Summer evening on a park near the Bund. Discreet tête-à-têtes beneath the ever-watchful eye of the Cultural Revolution.

101. 1971. Peking. A young soldier in the People's Liberation Army stands guard in front of the marble columns of the Great Hall of the People.

102. 1980. Peking. The Forbidden City. The Chinese no longer pose beneath Mao's portrait but next to a car the photographer provides. For a few *jiaos* they can have a picture of their unattainable dream.

End Papers: Peking, 1979. One of the *dazibaos,* or big character posters, covering the Democracy Wall.

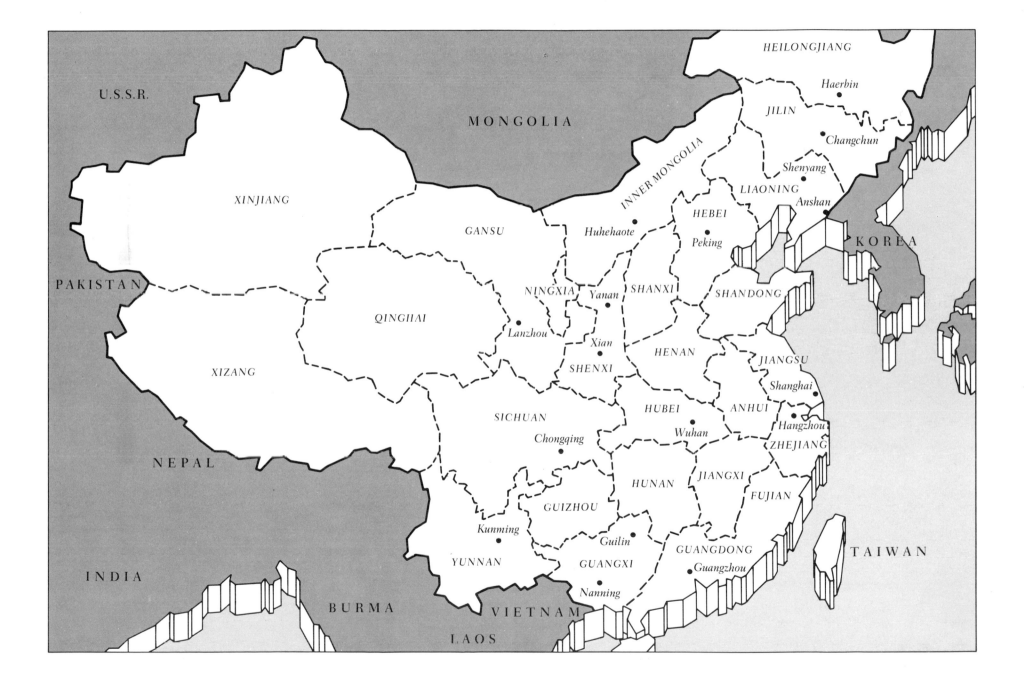

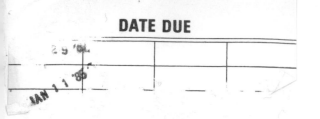
Marc Riboud, born in Lyon, France, in 1923, is a photographer long associated with Magnum. He has traveled as a photographer throughout the world, particularly in Asia. One of the first Europeans to enter China after the revolution, he spent four months there in 1957 and returned in 1965, 1971, 1979, and 1980. Mr. Riboud's photographs have appeared in major European and American magazines, and have been exhibited in New York, London, and Paris. Two previous collections of his work, *Three Banners of China* (1966) and *The Face of North Vietnam* (1972), were awarded the Overseas Press Club Prize. Mr. Riboud lives in Paris.

Orville Schell is the author of *"Watch Out for the Foreign Guests!": China Encounters the West* and *In the People's Republic,* co-editor of the first three volumes of *The China Reader,* and co-author of *Modern China.*